Early Pete Seeger Banjo Techniques

by Joseph Weidlich

ISBN 978-1-57424-405-2
SAN 683-8022

Special thanks to Tinya Seeger and the Seeger Estate

Photograph (cover): Pete Seeger performed at the 2005 General Assembly of the Unitarian Universalist Association
(© 2005 Allan Stern/UUA) used by permission.

Vega Pete Seeger model banjo photo by Sam Hirsh, Bernunzio Uptown Music.

TABLE OF CONTENTS

INTRODUCTION

Pete Seeger took an interest in playing the 5-string banjo when he was 16 years old after he heard it played by Samantha Baumgartner at the 1935 Asheville Folk Festival in North Carolina; he was immediately attracted to the sound of the instrument. As he was living in Washington, DC at the time he was fortunate enough to obtain an internship at the Library of Congress' Music Division which allowed him access to listen to a lot of folk music recordings in its holdings, some of which he also began to transcribe. It was also fortuitous that around that time banjoist Bascom Lamar Lunsford, who happened to be the organizer of the Asheville Folk Festival, visited Seeger's father; Pete managed to get a brief lesson from Lunsford where he learned the mechanics of what he would eventually call his Basic Strum. From then on Seeger made it a point to seek out, listen to and learn from any banjo players that he met in his travels, for example, Rufus Crisp of Allen, KY, learning a number of different playing styles along the way which he then experimented with to back up his vocals.

In early 1940 Seeger found himself in New York City where he joined a vocal group called The Almanac Singers which specialized in protest songs, primarily connected with the left-wing labor movement called The Popular Front. While they recorded several 78rpm "albums" that focused on songs reflecting this type of political material, e.g., union songs, protest songs, etc., they also recorded two albums of traditional folk music: one was called *Deep Sea Chanteys and Whaling Ballads* while the other was called *Sod Buster Ballads* (Folk Songs of the Early West). Both of these albums were recorded by folklorist Alan Lomax (son of noted musicologist John Lomax) on his General Records label. Allegedly, the rationale for making these two albums was the fact that they desperately needed $250 in order to buy a used car to drive out to California. When needs must, indeed!!

Here are the songs which they recorded on July 7, 1941 (the order presented here is based on the sequential recording master numbers):

Blow Ye Winds, Heigh Ho
Away, Rio
Blow the Man Down
House of the Rising Sun
Ground Hog
State of Arkansas
The Weaver's Song
I Ride an Old Paint
Hard, Ain't It Hard
The Dodger Song
Greenland Fishing
The Golden Vanitee
The Coast of High Barbary
Haul Away, Joe

As you will see, most of these songs are performed using the Regular C Tuning (gCGBD), a couple use the Open G Tuning (gDGBD), and some others employ altered tunings. Of course, **our interest in these recordings lie in hearing Pete Seeger's developing banjo style, as these recordings predate his first published banjo method by seven years (in 1948)**.

THE BASIC STRUM

The foundation of Pete Seeger's playing style is what he called The Basic Strum which is a pattern based on the shuffle rhythm of a quarter note followed by two eighth notes or an eighth note followed by two sixteenth notes:

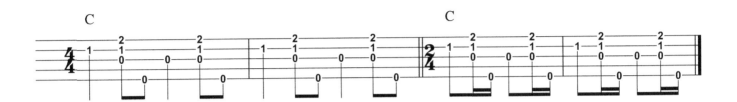

Pete Seeger modified the way that clawhammer banjoists play this rhythm, i.e., instead of playing the first note of the pattern with a down stroke with the index finger followed by a downward brush stroke with the index finger followed by the thumb playing the open fifth string he played the first note with an upstroke with the index finger (thus finger picking) followed by a downward brush stroke played by the middle and/or ring fingers followed by the thumb playing the open fifth string.

He coined the phonetic phrase used to describe this rhythm as *bumm-titty*. This rhythm had already been firmly established as one of the foundations in minstrel banjo performance technique by 1855, when the first published banjo method appeared, *Briggs Banjo Instructor*. Here is such an example used in the opening of the minstrel song *Old Dan Tucker*.

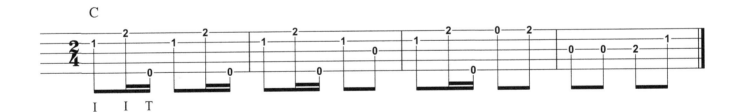

To demonstrate how important this pattern was here is a strikingly similar example, this time in the key of G, in the opening of the song *Walk Along, John*:

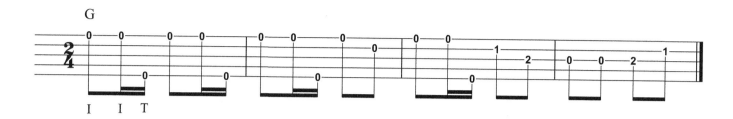

As you can see **this rhythmic lick is very versatile and you will see that Seeger used in all of the time in his banjo backups**. Incidentally, the minstrel banjoists didn't play brush strokes in the basic strum pattern as is common today. The use of their leaner sounding single brush strokes is still used today in the Round Peak style of clawhammer banjo performance. Later on I will show how Seeger also used this technique for songs played at faster tempi as well as adapting the IMT right hand fingering to this pattern.

Seeger frequently added a note between those beats, often using a hammer-on or pull-off, which could be rhythmically vocalized as *bum-pa-tit-ty*, or *Chatt-a-noo-ga*:

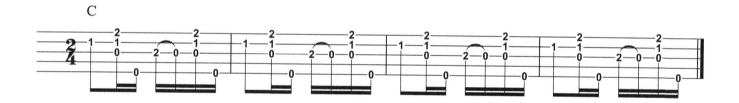

Another important technique in the playing of the minstrel banjoists was a note sequence that we refer to today as *double thumbing* because the thumb is used twice in the four note pattern on the weak beats. As you can see from the following example it is simply a rhythmic variation of The Basic Strum:

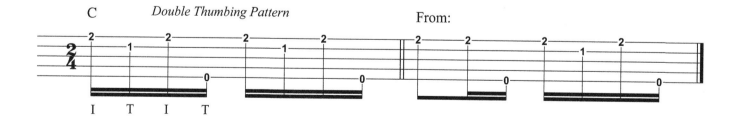

Let's look at a couple of examples of this usage from *Briggs Banjo Instructor*. The first is the opening of the song *Who's Dat A Knockin' At De Door*:

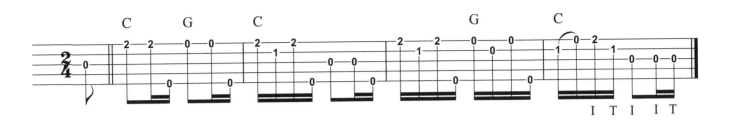

As you can see this technique creates a lot of forward motion. Now let's look at the opening of the B section of Briggs' arrangement of *Camptown Hornpipe*:

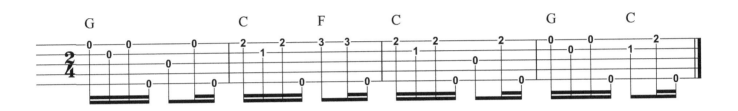

Interestingly, Seeger rarely used this double thumbing technique in his back-ups with The Almanac Singers in their 1941 recordings (one brief example can be found in his backup for the sea shanty *Blow Ye Winds, Heigh Ho*).

PERFORMANCE NOTES
ON THE ARRANGEMENTS

BLOW YE WINDS, HEIGH HO. This was the first song that The Almanac Singers recorded. Here is the tune, for those of you who don't know it:

Blow Ye Winds

They played it in the key of E flat so Seeger played it using Regular C Tuning (gCGBD) capoing his banjo at the third fret. Of course, this immediately created an issue with the tuning of the fifth string because if you tune that string higher than a whole step (from G to A) it will usually break. Seeger solved this problem by installing a small screw on his banjo's fingerboard immediately behind the 9th fret so that it acted as a capo. When that string was then set under the screw head the fifth string was automatically raised two whole steps, from G to B. As the fifth of the E flat chord is B flat all that he had to do then was to lower the tuning of the fifth string one-half step.

Here is how Seeger kicked off this sea shanty, in the down picking clawhammer style:

Blow Ye Winds, Heigh Ho

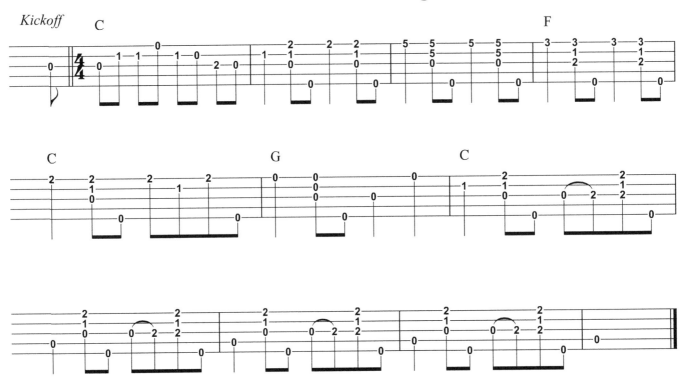

AWAY, RIO (aka **RIO GRANDE**). Here is the melody for this tune (incidentally, they pronounced *Rio* as "rye-oh"):

Away, Rio

This song is in triple meter and was played in the key of D so Seeger played it using Regular C Tuning capoing his banjo at the second fret. When playing in the key of D banjo players usually raise the tuning of the fifth string one whole step, from G to A.

Now, here was Seeger's kickoff:

Away, Rio

For his backup he used the rhythm that banjoists often play in 3/4 time:

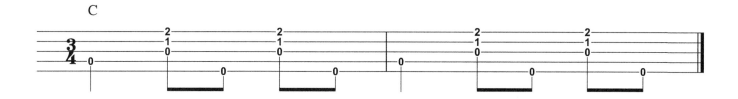

BLOW THE MAN DOWN. Here is the melody for this well known tune:

Blow the Man Down

The Almanac Singers recorded it in the key of C so Seeger played it using Regular C Tuning, no capo required. As you can see it is in 6/8 time; in songs like these Seeger often just played a single brushed chord keeping his right hand thumb on the fifth string so he could get a stronger sound with his downward brush stroke:

Blow the Man Down

HOUSE OF THE RISING SUN. This well known blues song was recorded in the key of D; Seeger used Regular C Tuning capoing his banjo at the second fret. Here is the vamp that set up the tempo for the song:

House of the Rising Sun

Opening Vamp

C

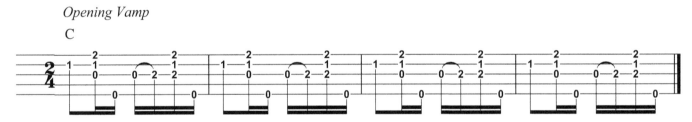

You might recall this backup pattern as it appeared in the section on The Basic Strum.

Now, here is the backup Seeger used in this tune:

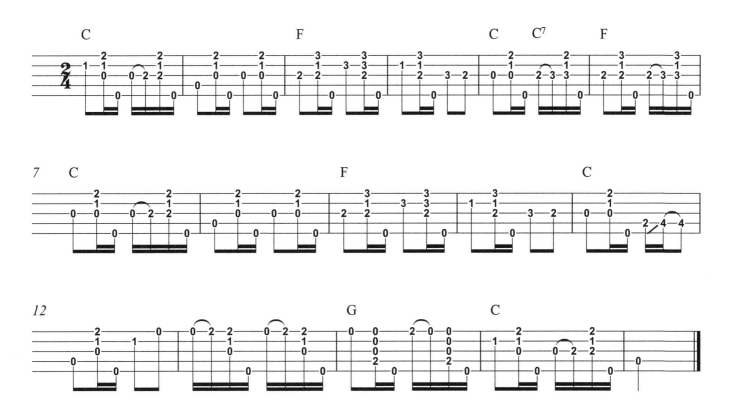

Make note of the voice leading over the F chord in measures 3 and 4 (introducing the sixth scale degree of the F scale) and the blues note sequence in the following measure over the C chord creating a C7 chord voicing: very ingenious, indeed.

Seeger would also often arpeggiate the F chord on the downbeat:

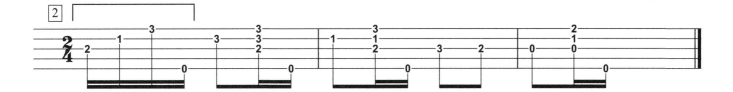

Now, here is Seeger's backup for the Outro which included a number of hammer-ons and pull-offs (note in particular the F6 chord voicing that I just discussed):

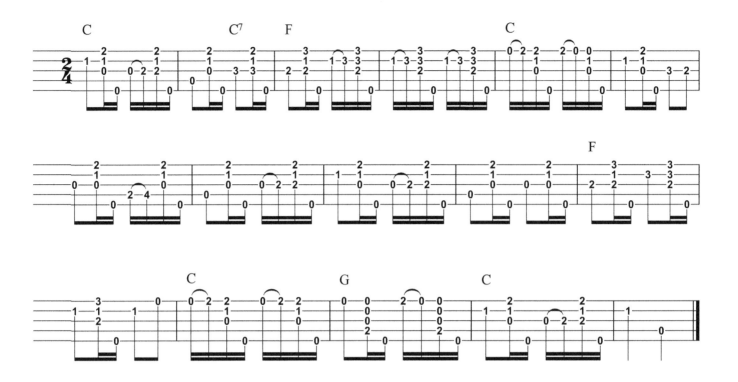

GROUND HOG. This is a well known country tune (and a crooked one at that!). The Almanac Singers played it in the key of G so Seeger used an Open G Tuning (gDGBD). Here is his basic backup:

Ground Hog

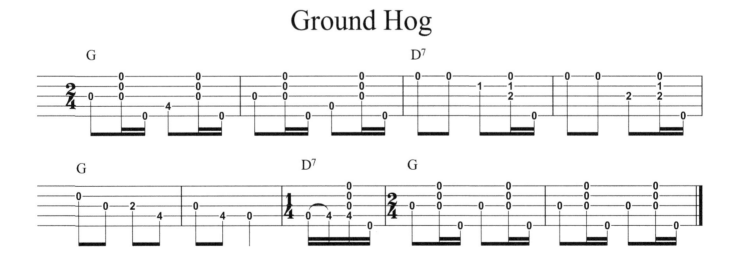

Here is a variation which Seeger played:

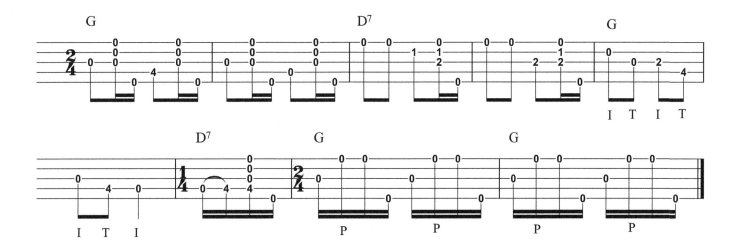

Note that he used an open string pull-off in the last two measures over the G chord.

STATE OF ARKANSAS. This song was recorded in the key of E so Seeger played it out of Regular C Tuning with his banjo capoed at the fourth fret with the fifth string positioned under the 9th fret fingerboard screw, thus raising it up two whole steps, from G to B:

State of Arkansas

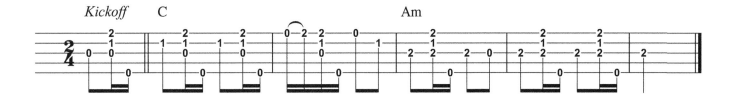

Seeger played several variations over the C chord between verses, acting as a bridge:

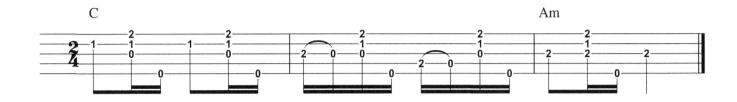

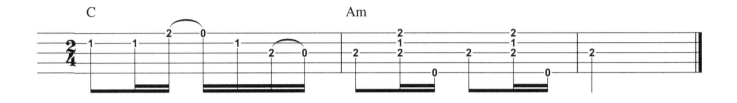

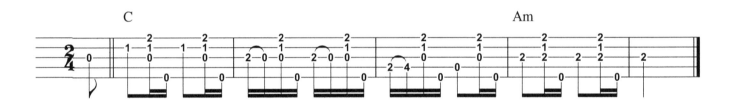

THE WEAVER'S SONG. This song was recorded in the key of D so Seeger used Regular C Tuning capoing his banjo at the second fret and tuning his fifth string up one whole step, from G to A. He played a number of different variations over the chords in between verses:

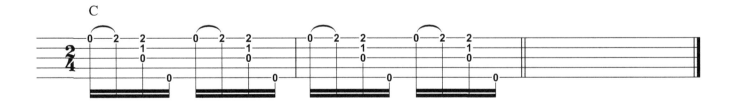

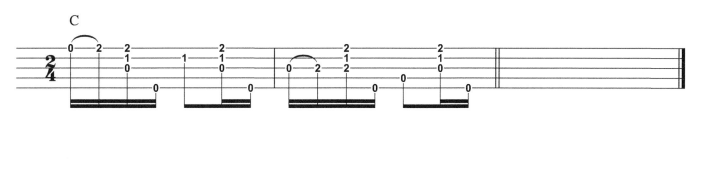

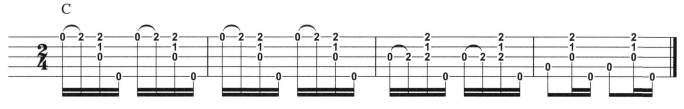

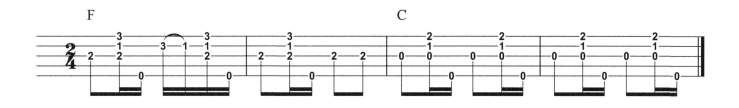

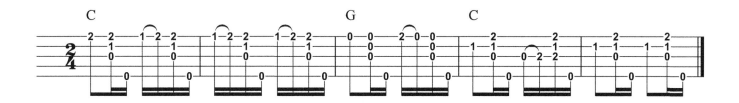

Here is Seeger's Coda backup lick for this tune:

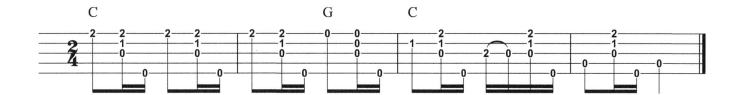

I RIDE AN OLD PAINT. Here is a classic cowboy song in triple meter. It was recorded in the key of E so, once again, Seeger played it out of Regular C Tuning with his banjo capoed at the fourth fret with the fifth string positioned under the 9th fret fingerboard screw, thus raising it up two whole steps, from G to B. Here is the introduction played by Seeger:

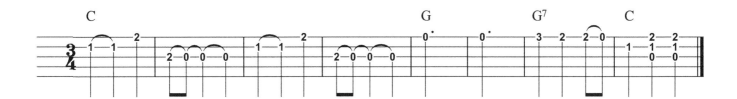

While he backed up the song using an alternating bass note pattern he also used a strummed backup over the C chord (again, you might want to keep your right hand thumb anchored on the fifth string as you do these strums):

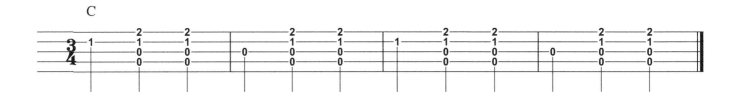

Bascom Lamar Lunsford

18

HARD, AIN'T IT HARD. This song was recorded in the key of D so Seeger used Regular C Tuning capoing his banjo at the second fret and tuning his fifth string up one whole step, from G to A:

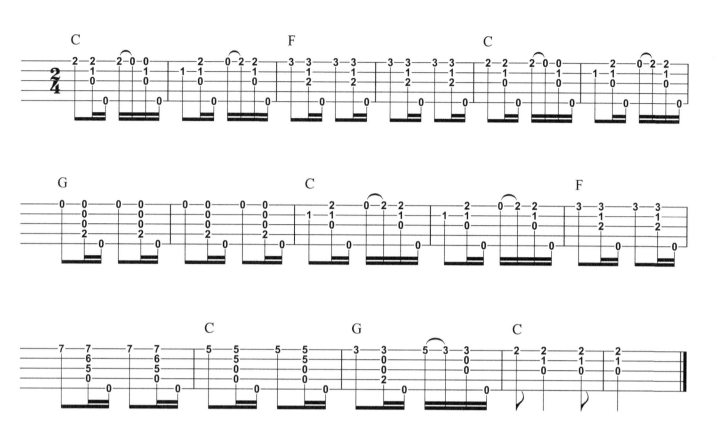

Pete Seeger

In his various backups behind the vocals Seeger voiced some of his chords differently so I have created a backup incorporating some of them:

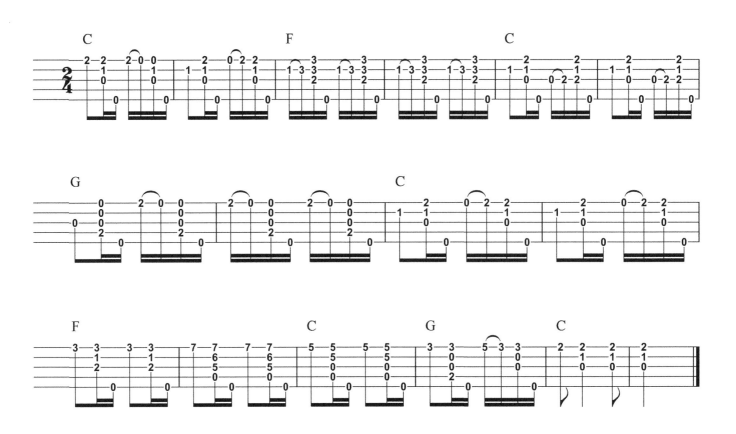

The Weavers

Now, here is how another way that Seeger arranged this song:

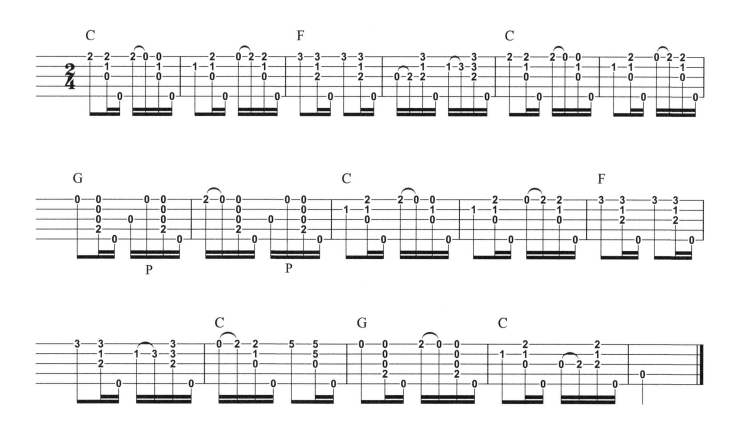

THE DODGER SONG. This song was recorded in the key of D so Seeger used Regular C Tuning capoing his banjo at the second fret and tuning his fifth string up one whole step, from G to A. You will immediately notice that he finger picked this kickoff:

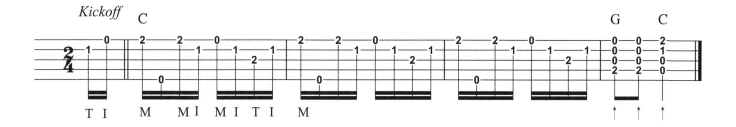

The C chord backup pattern Seeger played was similar to that which he used in the song *Hard, Ain't It Hard*:

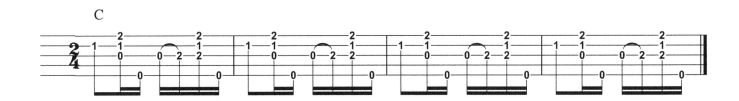

GREENLAND FISHING (aka **THE GREENLAND WHALE FISHERIES**). Here is the melody for this sea shanty:

The Greenland Whale Fisheries

The Almanac Singers recorded it in the key F so Seeger used an Open G Tuning but tuned his banjo down one whole step. Here is his basic backup (note the new right hand fingering in measures 2 and 3; it is the finger picked version of the down picking clawhammer technique, called Index Lead):

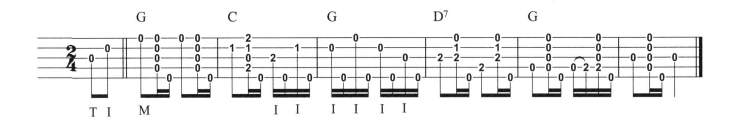

THE GOLDEN VANITEE. Here is the melody about the ship's crew hunting for whales:

The Golden Vanitee

This song was recorded in the key C so Seeger used Regular C Tuning. The back-up is similar to that as used in *The Dodger Song*:

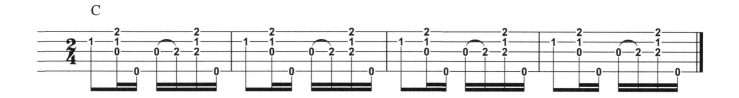

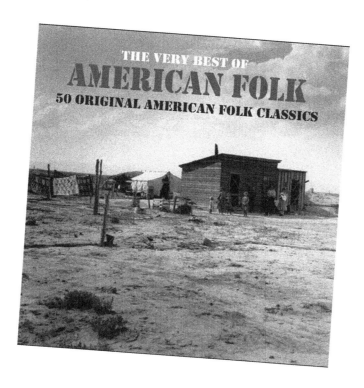

THE COAST OF HIGH BARBARY. Here is the melody:

The Coast of Barbary

This song was recorded in the key of F minor using the chord progression Fm – Cm- Bbm – C7 – Fm. You can actually use two different tunings to play this song. The first is to simply use the Regular C Tuning at concert pitch:

The Coast of High Barbary

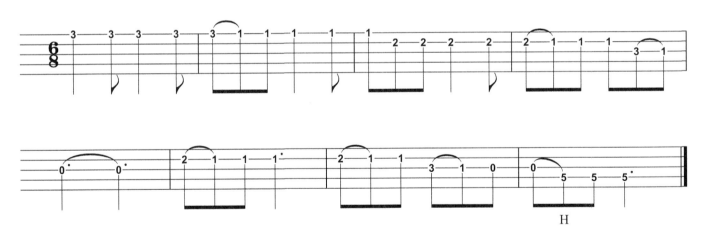

An alternate choice is to use a **minor tuning**. In the *Briggs' Banjo Instructor* it was mentioned that if the performer wanted to <u>play in a minor key</u> then he should tune the second string down one half step (that is, the third of the chord in Open G Tuning). In this particular instance, you would lower the pitches of Open G Tuning down one whole step to Open F Tuning and then lower the second string down an additional half step (from A to A flat) creating an F minor chord voicing (fCFAbC). If you use this tuning then you will find that the pull-offs lead to open strings for a more resonant sound:

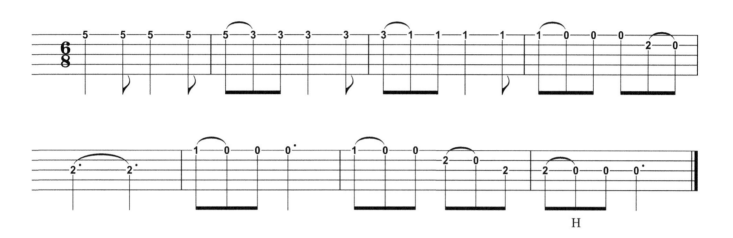

I believe that this is the tuning which Seeger used based on the alternating note backup that he played for the voicing of the F minor chord, as it could only be voiced using this altered tuning:

By the way, Seeger also used this minor tuning scheme in his arrangement of *Hush Little Baby* (in the key of G minor) found in his banjo method.

HAUL AWAY, JOE. This is the last song recorded by The Almanac Singers at their recording session. Here is the melody for this sea shanty:

Haul Away, Joe

It was recorded in the key of D minor so Seeger used Regular C Tuning. His back-up consisted of single chord strikes (similar to that used in *Blow the Man Down*); also, he kept his thumb on the fifth string so that it wasn't accidentally played creating an unintentional dissonance:

Haul Away, Joe

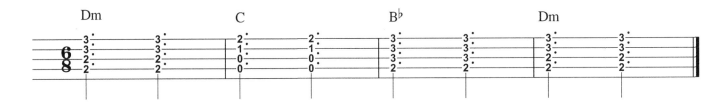

If you are familiar with Pete Seeger's banjo method, *How to Play the 5-String Banjo*, then you probably noticed that some basic idiomatic techniques are missing from these arrangements recorded by The Almanac Singers, for example, Thumb Lead and 3-finger picking. I will discuss these and some other techniques below.

EVOLVING TECHNIQUES

Now that I have presented the basic backups used by Pete Seeger in his July 1941 recordings with The Almanac Singers let's look at how he developed those basic techniques. The following examples all come from the recordings by The Weavers during 1949-1953 and their 1955 live performance at Carnegie Hall, as well as the text and tab extracts that accompanied Seeger's long playing (LP) recording from his 1954 banjo method on Folkways Records.

As I mentioned in the Introduction Pete Seeger made it a point in his travels to seek out, listen to and learn from the banjo players that he met. Over the years he also became interested in songs from different cultures, e.g., Calypso, Israeli, Indonesian, etc., so he developed different ways to play the rhythms indigenous to those cultures on the 5-string banjo.

THE BRUSHLESS BASIC STRUM. As it is difficult to cleanly play the basic strum at faster tempi Seeger began to eliminate the brush stroke by playing only the top note of the chord. Let's look at an arrangement of the folk song *Darling Corey*. He played it in the key of A flat using the Open G Tuning with his banjo capoed at the first fret, played in the clawhammer style. Please note that it is a crooked tune, i.e., there is an extra measure in the song.

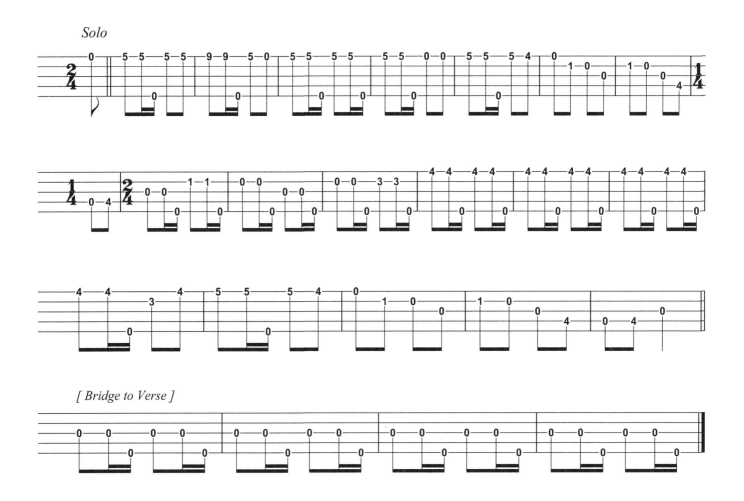

[Bridge to Verse]

During one of the verses Seeger played a 3-string style finger picking backup over a G chord instead of the expected basic strum pattern:

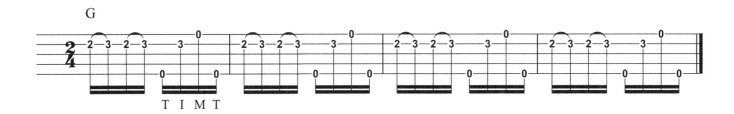

Of course, this lick is from Earl Scruggs' banjo solo *Foggy Mountain Breakdown* which he recorded with Flatt & Scruggs in late 1949. Pete Seeger says that he wasn't even aware of Earl Scruggs until 1950.

He also played this style of lick in the clawhammer style, also usually played at a faster tempo:

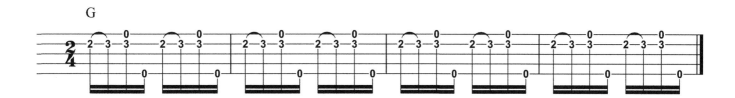

GUITAR STYLE FINGERINGS (IMT).

Using a "guitar style" of picking was not new to the banjo. For example, in the *Dobson Brothers' Modern Method for the Banjo* (1871) it is explained that in playing "guitar style" you should pick the first string with the second finger (M), the second string with the first finger (I) and that the thumb then plays the notes found on the remaining three strings.

Now, here is an example from this method that is played in first position:

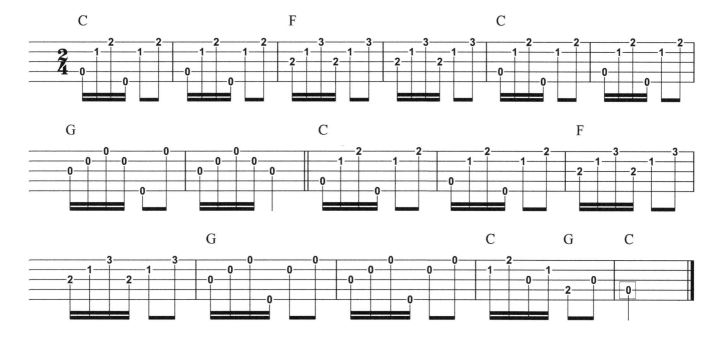

In the following tune, called *Little Mary Polka*, note that in the B section that some chords are played "up-the-neck":

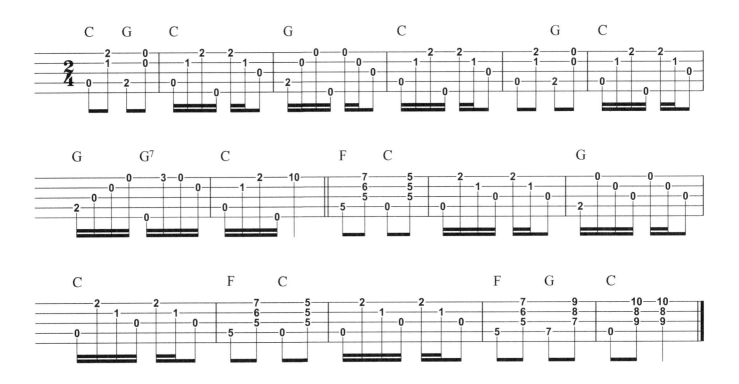

Here is an example of this "guitar style" of playing which Seeger used in the kickoff for the song *Kisses Sweeter Than Wine*, played it in the key of D using the Regular C Tuning capoing his banjo at the second fret:

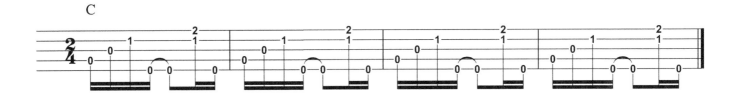

Seeger also experimented using the guitar style of fingering (i.e., IMT) in the shuffle rhythm of the basic strum:

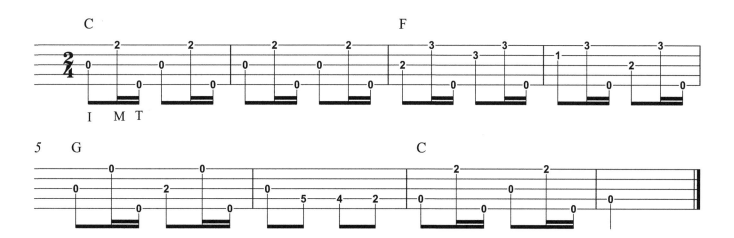

Seeger occasionally introduced **a counter melody** in his backups, as shown in the example below beginning at measure 9 (Regular C Tuning), again using the IMT fingering in the Basic Strum pattern:

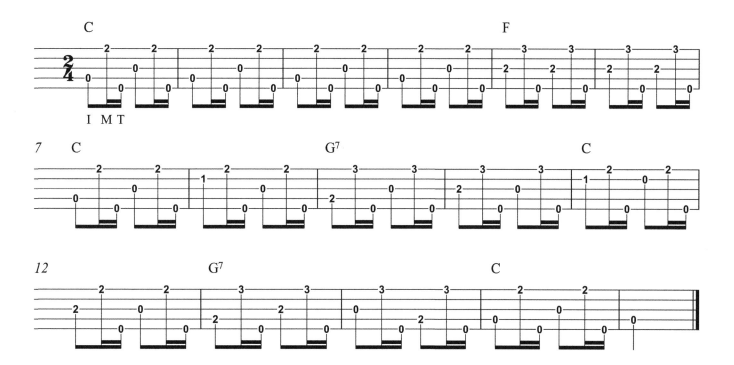

DOUBLE THUMBING TECHNIQUE. In the section on The Basic Strum I outlined an example of the technique called *double thumbing*. While Seeger rarely used it in the recordings with The Almanac Singers he did begin to incorporate it into his backups later on. For example, here is an arrangement of *Skip to My Lou* using this technique:

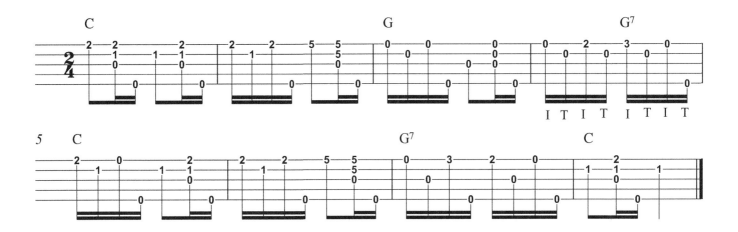

This arrangement is interesting in that he fitted in a moving scale line into the double thumbing lick. Tom Briggs also did this in the arrangements found in his 1855 *Banjo Instructor.*

THUMB LEAD STYLE. The Thumb Lead style evolved from what is called a pinch pattern, i.e., the first and fifth strings played together. The pinch could then be broken up with the fifth string being played first followed by the first string, and then a roll could be created by playing a secondary drone note on the first string. Here are those examples:

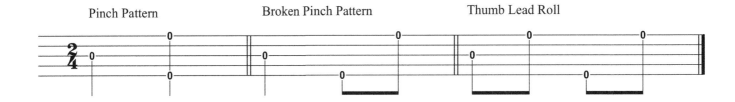

Of course, it is called Thumb Lead because the thumb "leads," or plays, the melody notes on the first and/or third notes of the roll. Here is the song *Skip To My Lou* using this technique played in the key of G Major (using Open G Tuning):

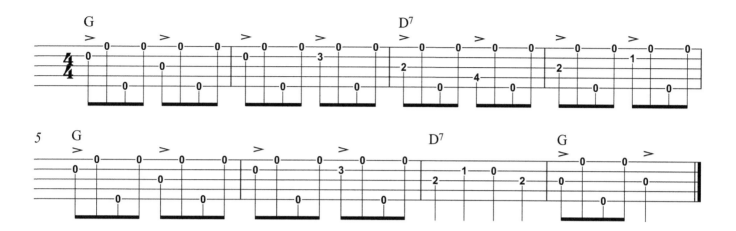

Some players prefer to play the first string with the middle finger, as it feels more natural; others prefer using the index finger.

Now, let's revisit the song *Hard Ain't It Hard* which Seeger also arranged in the thumb lead style using Open G Tuning; note that he incorporated a couple of open string hammer-ons:

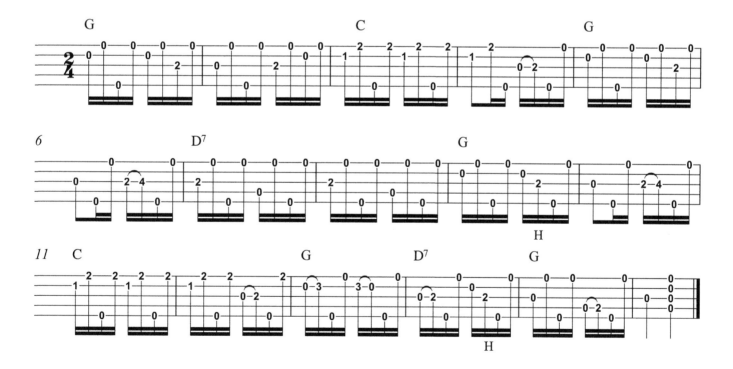

In the following song, recorded in the key of D using Regular C Tuning with his banjo capoed at the second fret, Seeger played the basic melodic line in the A section; in the B section, which modulates to the key of G Major, he seems to have played it using an intricate IMT fingering pattern instead of down picking the phrase:

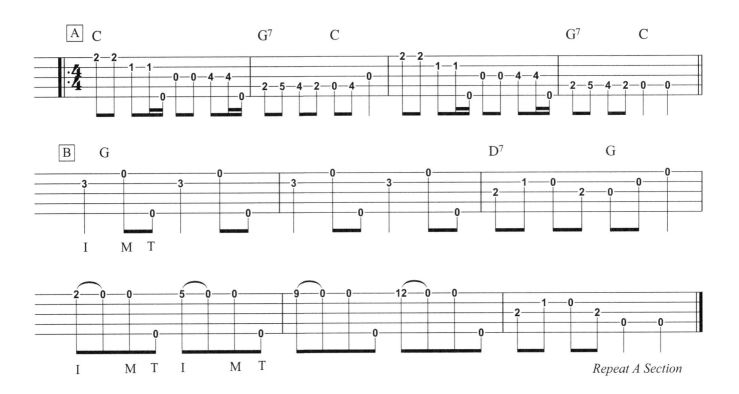

Seeger also played a second solo that featured the use of double stops (played by the index and middle fingers) followed by an ascending and descending scale line:

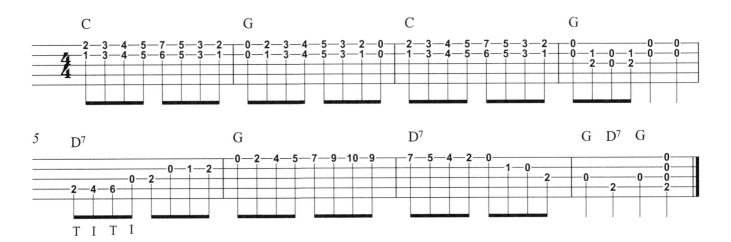

Since we just discussed double stops here is an example in 3/4 time in the key of D, using Regular C Tuning with the banjo capoed at the second fret, where the note sequences are played "up-the-neck":

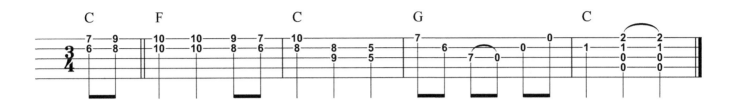

STRUMS. As we have seen, in a couple of the sea shanties in 6/8 meter Seeger strummed the chordal backups instead of using his basic strum. Here is a similar style of backup that he used for the African song *Wimoweh* which was recorded in the key of G flat using Open G Tuning, thus tuning his banjo down one-half step. It seems that he only used the index finger for the strums accenting the upbeats (where the chord changes). This is more easily played if you keep the right hand thumb on the fifth string as an anchor:

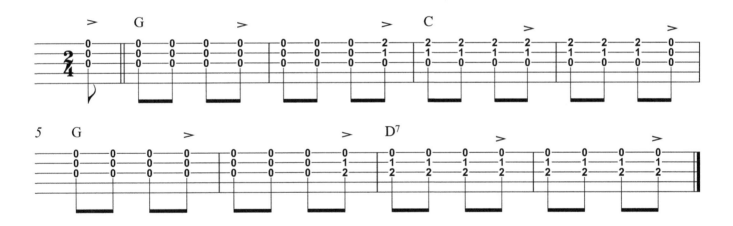

He also used this same technique in other backups, such as for the song *Follow the Drinking Gourd.*

Here is another example, this time using a tied note in the strumming pattern creating a syncopation. It is played using Open G Tuning; once again, keep right hand thumb anchored on the fifth string for a stronger strum:

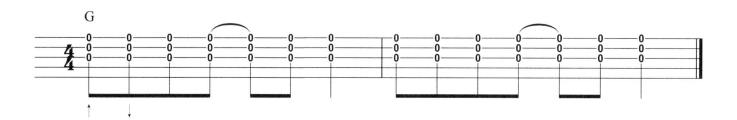

A syncopated style rhythm can also be used in a simple strum pattern. You might remember hearing this chromatic movement, as it was used earlier in *The Weavers Song*:

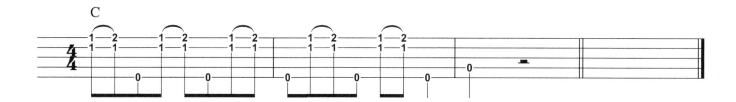

The following example also implies a 3-3-2 syncopation reminiscent of calypso rhythms:

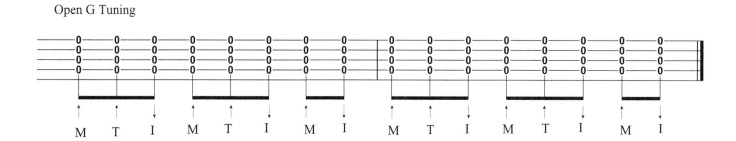

Here are a couple of other useful backup strums:

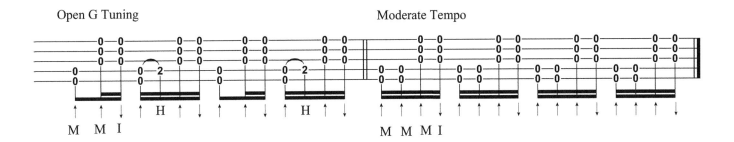

During the folk music era, ca. late 1950s through the early 1960s, the following strummed lick was often used between verses of a song (again, keep the right hand thumb anchored on the fifth string for a stronger brush stroke):

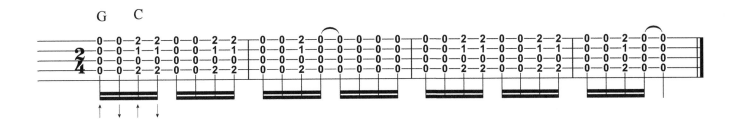

Here is a similar strum played over a G6 chord:

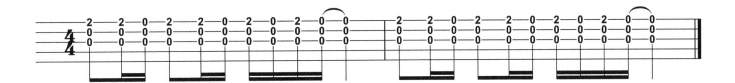

Pete Seeger

HOOKS AND LICKS.

Here is an interesting hook that Pete Seeger used to lead into songs in the key of G (using the Open G Tuning) such as the traditional railroad folk song, *The Rock Island Line*:

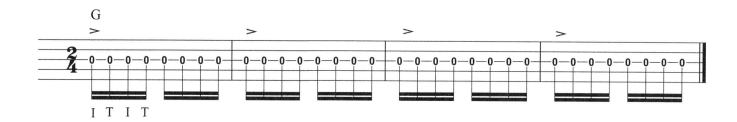

Seeger often played a slightly different lick between verses:

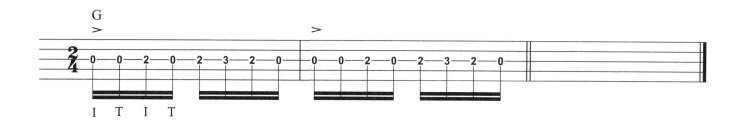

When this lick is played at a much faster tempo then it resembles a tremolo, as played on a mandolin. On the banjo this is best played by crossing the thumb over the index finger, like holding a flat pick, and then <u>rotating the wrist</u>, i.e., <u>do not</u> move the index finger as the effect then becomes ragged.

Let's look at a couple of other licks. First here is one in the key of G using the Open G Tuning which utilizes a tied note, creating a syncopation:

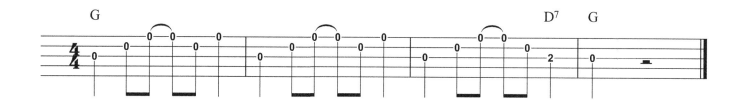

Meanwhile, the following lick in G is played out of an F chord shape at the third fret (using IMT guitar fingering):

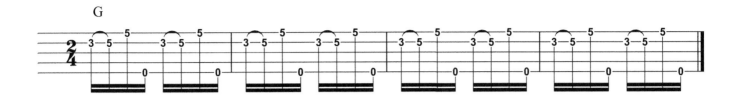

THE FORWARD ROLL. The forward roll is a syncopated note sequence played by the index finger, the middle finger, and the thumb (IMT) creating a 3-3-2 rhythmic pattern. The beauty of this roll is that you can easily leave out the last note of the roll, the second note of the roll, or both the second and eighth notes of the roll:

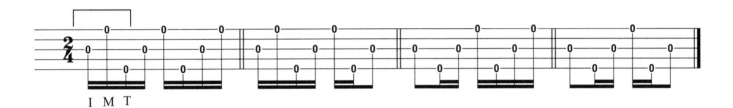

Earlier, the song *Skip To My Lou* was played using the Thumb Lead style; here I have arranged the first four measures of this tune using the basic forward roll pattern:

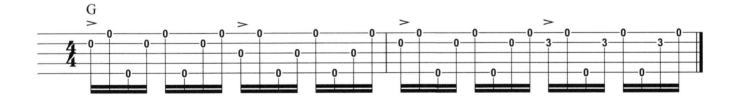

Now, here is Seeger's kickoff for the song *Hard, Ain't It Hard* played in the key of D using Regular C Tuning with his banjo capoed at the second fret. As you can see, this lick is played "up-the-neck":

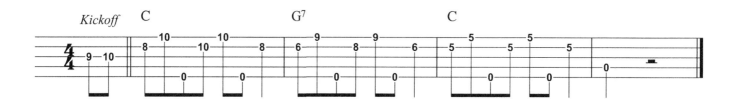

As a point of information, when the melody notes fall on the third and fourth strings then you can use a forward roll based on thumb lead: TIM TIM TM vs. IMT IMT IM:

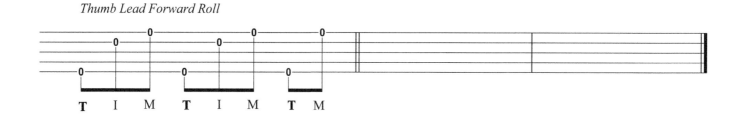

Here is an example of that usage, in Open G tuning, using an ascending pentatonic scale line on the fourth and third strings:

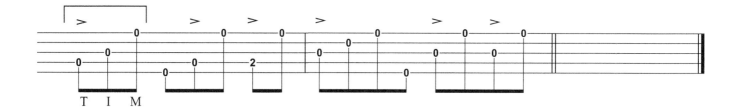

I think that it is appropriate to end this book with a solo that Seeger recorded in 1950 with The Weavers of their iconic universal protest song, *If I Had A Hammer* (aka *The Hammer Song*). As you can see, **he is really playing over the chord changes, not the melody,** using the double thumbing technique and the basic strum pattern (he played it in the key of C using the Regular C Tuning):

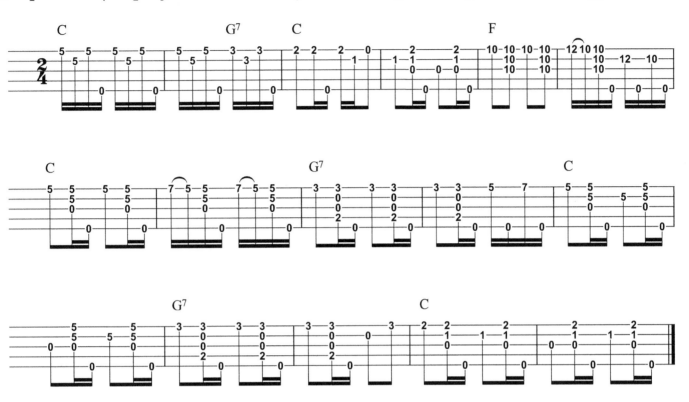

THE DEVELOPMENT OF THE LONG-NECKED BANJO

During his time with The Almanac Singers Pete Seeger found that when they played songs in the key of C he often felt that it would have been better if they had performed them one whole step lower, in B flat, as that key fitted his vocal range better. In order to do so he would have had to retune his banjo down one whole step, an inconvenience in concert performance. So, around early 1944 Seeger had a guitar builder extend his banjo neck by **adding two frets**; thus, he could now capo it at the second fret for Regular C Tuning and then take the capo off to play songs in the key of B flat without having to retune his banjo (except for the fifth string). This was a boon because he could now also play songs in the key of F using the Open G Tuning, doing the same thing.

In the early 1950s he decided to go one step further and have a banjo neck built with **three extra frets** (25 frets total) so that he could now also play songs in the key of A using the Regular C Tuning (having no need then to capo his banjo neck) and also play in the key of E in Open G Tuning as well (also uncapoed). This also provided him with different chord voicings as opposed to using a capo at the fourth fret on a standard 22-fret banjo neck to play in the keys of E. For example, when the song *Wimoweh* was performed by The Weavers in the key of G flat (1955 concert), all he had to do then was to lower his capo one fret (from the third fret to the second fret on his 25 fret banjo neck) and then retune his fifth string down one-half step as opposed to tuning all of the strings on his banjo down one half step. As it turns out this new, low "E" tuning (eAEG#B) was identical to that used by the early banjoists during the antebellum (pre-Civil War) period!

In any event, the Vega Company of Boston, MA, created the iconic Pete Seeger Long Neck Banjo model in early 1958. The rest, as they say, is history!

RELATED REFERENCE MATERIALS

Minstrel Banjo: Briggs' Banjo Instructor
Performance Notes and Transcriptions by Joseph Weidlich
Centerstream Publishing (1997)

Old Time String Band Banjo Styles
Performance Notes and Transcriptions by Joseph Weidlich
Centerstream Publishing (2013)
[Includes information on Bascom Lamar Lunsford]

The Almanac Singers: The Complete General Recordings
MCA Records (MCAD 11499)

5-String Banjo Instructor with Pete Seeger [1954]
Folkways Records (FI 8303)
Reissued by Smithsonian Folkways Archival
www.folkways.si.edu

More Great Banjo Books from Centerstream...

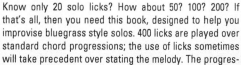